# THIS BOOK BELONGS TO
*The Library of*

..................................................................

..................................................................

# @COPYRIGHT 2024

The content contained within this book may not be reproduced, duplicated, or transmitted without direct written permission from the author or the publisher. Under no circumstances will any blame or legal responsibility be held against the publisher, or author, for any damages, reparation, or monetary loss due to the information contained within this book. Either directly or indirectly.

**Legal Notice:**

This book is copyright protected. This book is only for personal use. You cannot amend, distribute, sell, use, quote, or paraphrase any part, or the content within this book, without the consent of the author or publisher.

**Disclaimer Notice:**

Please note the information contained within this document is for educational and entertainment purposes only. All effort has been executed to present accurate, up-to-date, and reliable, complete information. No warranties of any kind are declared or implied. Readers acknowledge that the author is not engaging in the rendering of legal, financial, medical, or professional advice. The content within this book has been derived from various sources. Please consult a licensed professional before attempting any techniques outlined in this book. By reading this document, the reader agrees that under no circumstances is the author responsible for any losses, direct or indirect, which are incurred as a result of the use of the information contained within this document, including, but not limited to — errors, omissions, or inaccuracies.

Did you like my book? I pondered it severely before releasing this book. Although the response has been overwhelming, it is always pleasing to see, read or hear a new comment. Thank you for reading this and I would love to hear your honest opinion about it. Furthermore, many people are searching for a unique book, and your feedback will help me gather the right books for my reading audience.

Thanks!

## Table of Contents

| | |
|---|---|
| Foreword | 5 |
| 1. Body | 9 |
| Untitled | 125 |

**Discover the meaning, benefits and practical ways to take advantage of 127 key business buzzwords. Knowing and understanding these vital words will force a paradigm shift in the way you see business.**

If education is really power, this book is scientifically proven to give you superpowers.

---

It's one of the things we as humans hate to admit, that we don't actually know as much as we make others think we do. For the longest time I was living this dream that I was a businessman and an aspiring entrepreneur who will make millions in the future; 'watch me, I will'...was what I told people at school.

All I've ever wanted is to succeed, but although I was sure of it, I had no clue how it would actually manifest.

It was only when I started playing the game that is business and entrepreneurship, that I began to level up and move up the ranks.

What does 'the game' mean?

Well, I mean that business and entrepreneurship is a game both literally and figuratively - you might not know it yet, but you will. Unfortunately, it's not something that can be taught; only through your experience and practice will the game become more self-evident. Once you become conscious that it's a game with rules that must be understood, it's game over for the competitors.

Right now you're probably thinking:

"What the f*ck is this book all about? I've bought a book about business buzzwords and this guy is talking about business being a game! Show me some fancy words so I can learn!"

If you are thinking that, well done, you're learning already and although you aren't aware of it yet, you are already playing the game...you just haven't become conscious of it.

Why did you buy this book really? Don't worry this rant will all make sense shortly but for now, what are the main reasons you bought this book? To learn some new business lingo? Because you want to expand your knowledge? Because you want to be business savvy? Or is it because you recognize you need all the advantages you can get over your competitors if you want to be part of the 10% that succeed.

Maybe you've realized there's a hole in your game - a weak point, and that you lack the understanding of key business terms and principles, but, like me, you want to be a millionaire. You understand that education is quite literally the key to success. You know that the more you know, the more you can apply and the more you are able to communicate your business ideas, the higher the chance of you becoming successful. But, you recognize that you're still lacking knowledge and have no clue of some of the most basic business terms i.e. the meaning of having **ABSOLUTE ADVANTAGE.**

You don't have a major in business, and either you never went to university or didn't study business or entrepreneurship. You feel that you should be able to understand more business buzzwords to allow you to converse with other people in your business and during meetings. You want to feel and conduct yourself like a professional, not an impostor. This is a starting point.

You must put your ego to the side and learn and absorb knowledge if you want to become a successful businessman/woman. That's what your competitors won't tell you. People who are successful are constantly learning, they are constantly absorbing all the relevant information that will give them an edge.

That's part of the game.

Knowing more than others, but more importantly, applying and experiencing more than others by taking action.

So well done, you have started the game. You not only have taken action toward your goals, but you have also bought this book where you will discover all the key business buzzwords that are guaranteed to come up in a meeting, when listening to a podcast and when speaking to another successful business owner. You will also discover key business principles you must follow to ensure you become a success.

This is my selective pick of the business keyword I believe every entrepreneur should know.

Again, this is my personal selection of only relevant words. I am the owner of 2 six-figure online businesses and one seven-figure online business. I specialize in education and have done for the past 7 years. I only got to this point through the acquisition of knowledge and the application of it. Just knowing these words and principles changed how I viewed my business and I know it will change how you view yours too. I wish I had something like this when I was starting up, life would have been so much easier. But enough about me, this book is about you!

This book is about enabling you to acquire the relevant knowledge needed to dominate in your market. I'm not going to inform you of words you simply don't need to know, or irrelevant principles, as they won't take you closer to your goals.

By reading this book, you will gain a deep insight into business keywords and their benefits. You will also get a breaking of the fourth wall with certain words. I will provide you a personal BOSSNOTE on my thoughts and how you should apply yourself. As I said in the description, this is not a dictionary so don't read it like that, that's why there's no table of contents. This is (roughly) in alphabetical order and must be read chronologically. I would recommend you read it at night before bed so you can fully absorb and sleep on your newfound understanding of business terminology and lingo.

Of course, I have no control over how you read it, however I'll tell you the best way to get the most from this gold mine. This is book one of three of the millionaire playbooks. After you read this, you are one step closer to your business goals. You will be able to confidently express and articulate yourself.

So, if you're ready to absorb wisdom, let's begin.

A/B Test

A/B testing is also known as split testing in the online world. It's a simple process where you test two variants of the same webpage, ad banner, cover, or title of an ad that you are going to promote.

Running an A/B test means you are identifying which variant drives more conversions. You can then use the winning variant in your scale campaign, with confidence the campaign will do well.

**BENEFITS:** *Optimize your promotion*, meaning *higher conversion rate* and *less money spent* on advertisement.

# ACQUI-HIRE

When you are starting up a business and begin to build a team of devoted hardworking individuals, this acquisition process is known as acqui-hiring.
So, acqui-hiring is the process of building your team.

**BENEFITS:** You can build *trust*, a great *support system* around you and a *collective shared goal* within your chosen team.

# ALPHA RELEASE

The alpha release is the release process of a product that remains incomplete. This product, whether digital or physical, is given to a group of people who act as 'testers' and use and examine the product before it's finalized.

**BENEFITS**: *Enables rigorous testing* of a product before it goes to the mass market. It *allows for quality control*, as the product developers can implement feedback given by the testers ensuring the optimum final product. If it's a software product, alpha release helps *identify bugs.*

# ACCESSIBILITY

This just means how easily can your product, whether digital or physical, can be reached. Maybe through an app, a website, or at a physical store. Can your product be easily accessed?

**BENEFITS:** If you have a product that's easily accessible, this is great - it means your *target audience can easily buy and use* *your product* with ease, which means more sales and more money in the bank.

*If your product is online*, amazing - it means it's **accessible to near enough everyone online**. This doesn't mean everyone will buy or use your product, it just means that anyone who is interested in your product can reach it if they have access to the internet.

## ACCELERATOR

A business accelerator is a program that enables start-up companies to have ease of access to investors, mentorship from experienced business owners, and other support. This helps the business become self-sustained (no need for outside help in satisfying one's basic needs). These programs can last up to six months.

**BENEFITS:** Accelerator programs help businesses ***move past the early stages of the start-up***, helping the business become ***more established*** in its respected field. These programs also help ***connect businesses to the network*** of their peers.

# APPRECIATION

The general increase in the value of an asset over time. This is the opposite of <u>***depreciation:***</u> decrease in value of asset over time.

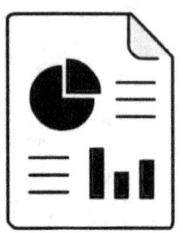

# ANALYTICS

This is the evidence-based computational analysis of a business's collected data and statistics. This often means looking at the business's past data in order to gain a better understanding of how to improve certain areas.

Whilst looking at analytics are you looking out for stand out KPI (**Key Performance Indicators**) this is used by business to judge the performance, progress and targets.
Within analytics, the KPI which are examined are:

***Acquisition cost:***

Total expenditure when obtaining a new client, worker or asset.

## *Return on investment:*

ROI aims to measure the amount a certain investment returns over time.

## *Customer lifetime value:*

How much value a customer provides a business for the entirety of their relationship.

## *Monthly recurring revenue:*

The recurring monetary value that a subscription-based business gets monthly. This definition works for any other time scale, such as annually - annual recurring revenue.

---

## *Units of product sold per day:*

The amount of product sold on a daily basis.

## *Conversion rate of landing page:*

The total number of sales divided by the total number of page visitors.

## *Advertising, marketing, and promotional costs:*

The total amount of money spent on promotion of a product, or on increasing brand awareness.

### *Adaptive expectations:*

This is the theory of how individuals shape their views about the future, using past trends and the errors of their own previous predictions.
An example of this would be predicting that 'the state of inflation has increased this year, therefore, it will increase next year'.

# ABSOLUTE ADVANTAGE

This is the easiest way to determine the economical performance of a business company. If one business is able to produce more of something with the same amount of effort and resources as another business, then that business has an absolute advantage.

To make things clearer; let's say you have two fashion design businesses, **A and B.** Each has the same number of individuals in their teams and have access to the exact same information and resources. However, business **A** by chance, has a far more creative team.
This means business **A** has an absolute advantage!

They are able to produce more high quality products with the same amount of resources.

Absolute advantage is relative to the respective business so the same principles which gave the business, for example, *'creativity',* might not allow for absolute advantage in another market.

**BENEFITS:** I feel this one's self-explanatory...but I'll give you a hint it's in the name. ;)

# ASSET

An asset is a useful, valuable thing that is the property of an individual person or company. ***Assets are characterized by growth,*** but not limited to financial growth.

**Examples of assets:**

Property/Land

Equipment

Trademark/Patent

Furniture

Inventory

# ADAPTIVE INDIVIDUAL

A person who is able to quickly change their approach, behavior or techniques to meet the requirements of their business environment, conditions, and landscape. They are able to learn new skills relatively quickly and have the ability to take in new information and apply their knowledge.

**BENEFITS:** Once again, it's self-explanatory.

**BOSSNOTE:** *Being able to adapt is probably the most important characteristic an entrepreneur needs to succeed.*

# BOOTSTRAPPING

Bootstrapping is the process in which an entrepreneur uses their own savings in combination with their experience, skills and knowledge to start and grow their business without capital.

**BENEFITS:** Bootstrapping forces you to be *more creative* with your ideas. It puts you in a position where you gain *experience in how to handle money* within your business efficiently. You also have *complete ownership* of your company, so you don't have to answer to investors - or look for them.

# BETA RELEASE

This is the next process of production, after your initial alpha release you then have beta release. This entails that you offer your product to your potential customer. They have time to use the product and will provide feedback. This feedback helps you understand where changes need to be made.

**BENEFITS:** Giving your potential customer your product to try before it's available to the mass market is amazing for ***quality control*** for your product. It gives you ***confidence that you've got the best product***. It also means you've done testing, so you know whether your product is ***consumer friendly.***

# BOARD OF DIRECTORS

Board members are individuals who act as mentors and advise business owners on the best practices and ways to run their business, through experience and knowledge. Oftentimes, these select few are also shareholders in the business.

Board of directors can be people who help with the hiring process, business development and fundraising. This all general oversight management of the business.

**BENEFITS:** They can provide *great guidance* in what direction the business should go. If you have a great team and support system they can help you *broaden your vision* and help you *attain your long term goals.*

**DRAWBACKS:** All these benefits are *relative to the board of directors*. If you have a great team then things are great. If you don't, then you are *potentially halting the progress of your business*. Finally, your board of directors may *not be on board with your vision* and *increase pressure* for you to deliver.

**BOSSNOTE:** Think carefully about the people you let in your inner circle, make sure they are on board with your vision, your brand and have crazy work ethics. Make sure you constantly surround yourself with positive, hardworking, passionate people.

There's a saying: **'You are a combination of the 5 people you spend most of your time with'** . Well, your business is quite literally its own entity and the product of the team that makes it up.

# BUSINESS DEVELOPMENT

This is the long term process of creation of value from an organisation, customer and market. This is essential to the role a business plays in its early stages of creation.

# BUSINESS MODEL CANVAS

This is the template start up companies use to structure their plan of action for the business and how they approach things. This is the strategic management of how the business will run.

This is also known as the BM template. Each business model has its own specialised model, with its own ins and outs.

*Variables that dictate a business model*

Source of revenue: *online business or offline business?*
Target audience: *young adults or the elderly?*
Product

**These are the four types of business models:**

**BUSINESS TO CONSUMER**

**BUSINESS TO BUSINESS**

**CONSUMER TO BUSINESS**

**CONSUMER TO CONSUMER**

# BURN

This is a term which is often used by investors. 'How much will you burn in the upcoming months?' This term simply means how much money one spends within a given period.

# BACK END

Back end departments or offices are functions in a business that provide the services that allow businesses to function.

**This includes:**

Administration

Accounting

Document handling

Communications data processing

Personnel (HR or human resources)

**Sly comment:** So for the most part the boring stuff. You can see this as the maintenance of your business. The things you absolutely should do but bore you to f*ck.

# BUSINESS EXPENSE

Business expenses are costs incurred in the ordinary course of business. They can apply to small entities or large corporations. Business expenses are part of the **income** statement. On the **income** statement, business expenses are subtracted from revenue to arrive at a company's taxable **net income**.

# BRANDING

Branding is seen as promotion of a particular product or company by means of advertising and distinctive design. Branding also means the message which you as a business owner are trying to send out. Brands represent things, even emotions. For example, one of the most recognisable brands in the world, Coca-Cola, tries to represent and is heavily associated with happiness and joy. Coca Cola literally translates to *'Tasty Fun'* or *'Delicious happiness'* in Mandarin.

## Benefits:

Strong customer recognition

Competitive edge in the market

Immense customer loyalty and shared values

Drastically increase profit margins. A trusted brand will always win customers over one that isn't, even if the product is exactly the same.

Increases the credibility of a product and thus makes it easier to sell.

## DRAWBACKS: NONE

**BOSSNOTE:** Building a strong brand goes a long long way. I know from experience, having started multiple businesses in different respected fields, I can strongly say the one myself and my customers are most connected to is the business with the strongest brand identity. People love to stand for something and be part of something great. I realised that they actively seek this out through brands.

**Why do you think clothing brands are so successful?**

They understand the power of branding and can charge ridiculous amounts for a piece of clothing. Most people buy not for the clothing itself, but for the feeling the clothing provides them - they are buying the brand! This same logic can be applied to near enough anything.

**YES, IT WILL TAKE YOU TIME. BUT THAT TIME IS WELL INVESTED.**
**THAT'S MORE MONEY IN YOUR POCKET IN THE FUTURE.**

# BONDS

Bonds are a different way to raise capital and an individual. It's seen as a safer alternative to selling shares or taking out a bank loan. They're regarded as a lower risk investment. Like shares in listed companies, once they have been issued, bonds may be traded on the open market. A bond's yield is the interest rate (or coupon) paid on the bond divided by the bond's market price.

**BENEFITS:** Bonds are *less volatile and risky* when compared to stocks. If they are held for an extended period of time, they can provide a *stable* but more importantly *consistent return on investment.*
Bonds also tend to have a *higher interest rates* when compared to banks.

# BEHAVIOURAL ECONOMICS

This is the study of biases, tendencies and heuristics which influence individuals' decisions to improve, tweak or overhaul traditional economic theory. Studying behavioural economics helps us determine whether people make good or bad choices and whether they could be helped to make better choices.

**BOSSNOTE**: I would recommend you look further into studies about this, analyse and reflect whether you're making emotive decisions or whether you are making rational decisions based on logic, facts and collected data, within your respective business.

**Case studies** have shown that people often overestimate the extent in which certain things in their business can be predicted. Studies have also shown that people are disproportionately influenced by a fear of feeling regret, and many people are engaged with business activities so they don't feel like they have failed.

# BARRIER TO ENTRY

**Barrier to entry** is an economics and **business** term alluding to factors which may regulate, and prevent newcomers into a market or industry sector. This regulation can enforce limited competition.

### What are different types of barrier to entry?

High start-up costs

Regulatory hurdles

Patent/trademark

Geographical barriers

Brand loyalty

Creative talent

**BENEFITS:** Barriers to entry helps regulate and protect the market. Barriers of entry are great as it means not everyone can succeed in a certain field. You need certain skills, knowledge, and backgrounds to enter certain fields. This might sound like a bad thing, but in all businesses, lower competition is always a good thing. If you have all the tools you need to enter a business then the barrier to entry helps you tremendously, if it protects your market from everyone else.

**BOSSNOTE**: View this the same way we are grateful for barriers to entry for doctors. You should be grateful that not everyone is able to start a business, as some businesses, even with a barrier to entry, are poorly run and looked after. You want a market which is able to produce the best functional business for society as a whole.

Before you enter any business venture, make sure to research the barrier to entry. The more niche you choose, if you join a business with a high barrier to entry, you'll have low competition. So, if you're successful, you'll be making a fortune, comfortable knowing competition is limited.

# BREAKEVEN

Is the point at which both expenses and revenue are of equal value, cancelling each other out so there is no net loss or gain. One has "broken even".

Most start-up businesses typically take 2 years to break even.

Copyright is a type of intellectual property that gives its owner the exclusive right to make copies of a creative work, usually for a limited time.
The creative work may be in a literary, artistic, educational, or musical form.

**BENEFITS:** You get ownership. You are able to enforce copyright laws if someone uses your work without permission. It protects creators, and business men and women.

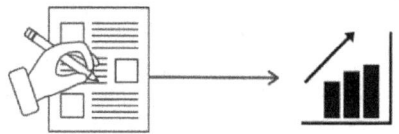

# COPYWRITING

The act of writing text and copy for the purpose of advertising. Copywriting is seen in the entrepreneurial world as a skill which must be developed. This is essentially persuasive language/writing used to show a potential customer the benefits of a product and why they would be stupid not to buy it. Within the 'copy', they aim to hit certain pain points of the target audience, invoking strong emotions.

**Things good copywriting should be:**

**URGENT:** Buy now - discount price ends in 24 hours

**UNIQUE:** Should come from a different angle

**USEFUL:** It should be informative about the product and its benefits

**ULTRA SPECIFIC:** Give time frame, exact price and stats

**EMOTIVE:** It needs to hit the reader's pain points and resonate with them.

**CLEAR:** Simple words with clear communication. It should be very easy to read.

**BENEFITS:** Good copy, which means a good written advertisement, can *increase conversions* of landing pages, meaning more money, more sales, and more traffic.

# CUSTOMER RETENTION

Customer retention refers to the actions and activities companies and organizations take to reduce the number of customer defections. Businesses tend to have customer retention programs in place subconsciously. They aim to help businesses retain as many customers as possible, often through customer loyalty and brand loyalty initiatives.

This could be giveaways, shoutouts, discounted prices for customers who have been with the business for a long time.

### BENEFITS:

Your **brand will stand out** from the crowd.

You will make **more money** due to word of mouth referrals.

You will have an overall **increase in individual customer lifetime value.**

You will **receive better feedback**, which will enable you to make **positive changes** to your business.

You can **build a strong, long lasting relationship** which at times, can be the driving force of your business.

**BOSSNOTE**: That last point is so important, I say this as the owner of a publishing business and other online businesses. Although my passion takes me 50% of the way there, it's the built relationship with the customer that takes me the whole way there. I feel more obliged to work harder than ever, to produce high quality products as it's my customers and now friends who I care for that I am trying to provide with quality products.

It keeps me motivated, it keeps me focused, and it pushes me to go that extra mile and do some extra research to ensure everything is up to scratch.

# CUSTOMER LIFE CYCLE

The customer life cycle is the process your customers go through when they are building a relationship with your business, from the point of initial contact.

# CUSTOMER ACQUISITION

This is the process of a business getting a new customer.

# CAPITAL

Capital is usually cash or liquid assets which are held or obtained by an individual of business for expenditures. In financial economics, this term can be expanded to include a company's capital assets.

# CAPACITY

The capacity of a business is the maximum output level of products that can be sustained while delivering a product or service. Most businesses try to understand and manage their capacity.
Capacity of each business is completely different and unique to that particular business.

# COLLATERAL

An asset which is seized from a borrower by a lender. Lenders tend to cause collateral to retrieve the value of a loan. This happens if the borrower fails to meet the arranged interest charges or payments.

# COMMODITY

A raw material or primary agricultural product that can be bought and sold, such as copper or coffee. Commodities are normally purchased in bulk.

Other commodities include things like, oil, cotton cocoa or silver. It can also be things which are manufacturer products like microchips and other computer resources.

# CUSTOMER RESEARCH

Customer research is the process of spending time discovering what one's target audience likes, what their pain points are, why they would relate to the business, what motivates then, and what their buying behaviour is like. Customer research allows a business to deeply understand their client and consumer base. The clearer you are about who your target audience is, the better you can direct your efforts in product, advertising, marketing and pricing.

**Here are some simple ways to carry out customer research:**

Interviews

Online surveys

Living in the online environment your potential customer might be in

For example, if you have a business that sells products to dog owners, although dog owners are a huge variety of ages, the majority age range would be middle age or older, right? Now what platform would they most likely be active on?
Tiktok? Instagram?
Facebook?

So now that you have identified the platform they spend most of their time on. What next?

You can either join already existing dog related Facebook groups and begin networking, reaching out to people and connecting. You can see what sort of stuff they post and what gets the most likes which give you a better view on what they like and what they are like.

The next step would be to create your own Facebook 'Dog Lover's' group, maybe make it niche, 'Middle aged women bulldog lovers group' - the more specific the better. You only want **a piece** of the market, this makes things easier to handle. Anyway, now that you have that group, you can ask questions, interact and provide value. Over time you will gain a better understanding of your customer's behaviours, pain points, motivators and buying habits.

*Trust me, I have done more customer research than you can imagine. It is a process that happens everyday. Business is never static. Things are always moving forward and if you slack just for a moment, competition will take over. A great way to get absolute advantage is by knowing your customer more than your competitors. Simple.*

## Here are just a few benefits of customer research:

Minimises investment risk

Uncovers and identifies potential problems

Identifies holes in the marketplace

Better understanding of what the customer wants

Strategic planning for the future

**THROUGH YOUR CUSTOMER RESEARCH, YOU CAN CREATE A CUSTOMER AVATAR.**

# CASH FLOW

Cash flow is the net amount of cash and equivalents being transferred into and out of a business.
When a business is able to create sufficient value and is able to generate positive cash flow, this tends to be the time that investors want in.

**BENEFITS:** Again, self explanatory.

# CAP TABLE

This is essentially a spreadsheet which documents a business's shareholders, investors, ownerships, equity shares and similar.

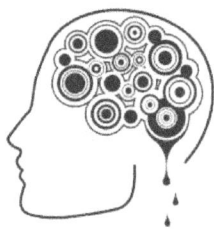

# CREATIVE MIND

This is the mind of a person that is able to see the world in a different way. In relation to business it refers to an individual's mind who is able to come at a business model with all the same information but is able to come at it from an entirely different angle which yields lots of benefits, whether that's making higher sales, making the system more efficient, or making customer acquisition a breeze.

A creative mind is able to solve problems quicker than the average person as they are not confined by rules. They can take a step back and think outside the box, they can see the bigger picture and make links others can't.

**BENEFITS:** This is a ***skill which can be developed over time***, and gives you an ***advantage over your competitors***. Creativity means you can ***solve problems faster,*** with less brain power.

Business is us constantly solving problems, and making links other people can't. When we do that, we succeed. When we do that, we get paid!

# COMPOUND INTEREST

Compound interest is the interest you earn on interest.

Here's a quick example:

Let's say **$100** is in a bank account with an interest rate of **10% a year.**

At the **end of the year,** the account will contain **$110.**

If the **money is left** in the account untouched, **10%** interest will be **paid on the $110.**

Meaning in the **second year you will have $11** interest added, making **$121.**

**BOSSNOTE:** I'll leave you with a quote from **Albert Einstein:** *'Compound interest is the eighth wonder of the world. He who understands it, earns it; he who doesn't, pays it.'*

# DEBT

Debt is an amount of money borrowed by one party from another. Debt is used by many corporations and individuals as a method of making large purchases that they could not afford under normal circumstances.

**BOSS NOTE:** It's a common misconception that debt is bad. This is wrong, debt is neither inherently a good thing or bad thing.

Debt is only as good or as bad as the person who takes it on. If you're an educated banker, businessman, corporation, government or real estate agent and understand the ins and outs of debt and how to use it to your advantage, then great.

However, if you're a person that lacks understanding of the ins and outs of debt but love getting the newest fashionable clothes and accumulating debt with the use of your credit card knowing you can't uphold the payback instalments, maybe debt isn't for you.

*It must be noted that I am not a financial advisor, just a well educated, successful businessman.*

Always do your own personal research. I would love to go into more detail about this topic but I simply can't as that's not the purpose of this book. The purpose of this book is to educate you as an entrepreneur on the most prevalent terms in business, equipping you with a solid understanding of the market and all the processes in running a business.

# DIVIDEND

When a corporation earns a profit or surplus, it is able to pay a proportion of the profit as a dividend to shareholders. So dividend means the sharing/distribution of profits with shareholders of a business, once the business is well into profit.

Any amount not distributed is taken to be re-invested in the business, called **RETAINED EARNINGS.**

It's worth knowing that the owner of the business can also pay themselves a dividend!

# DEMAND

The demand refers to the amount/volume of product that people are both willing and able to buy.
If a product is in high demand, it's a popular product and people want and are willing to pay the right price for it. In business we are always looking for products which are in high demand as this allows us to make the most amount of profit. It also means we can scale our business to the next levels.

**BOSS NOTE:** It is worth noting that the market chooses the demand of a product or service, and demand of a certain product can change over time. It's dynamic, not static. This just means the demand can increase or decrease at any time. However, there are certain things and evaluations that can be made to give you a clear idea of market trends and the direction things are heading in.

For example if you are working in Amazon FBA and you're selling Christmas products, understanding that the demand for your product is determined by seasonal changes, you are able to spot the trend that the demand for your products will increase from October onwards till the 24th of December at which point you expect the trend for the demand of your seasonal product to reduce.

Understanding trends will help you understand demand.

# DEMOGRAPHIC

Demographics can be seen as the collection and analyzation of broad characteristics about groups of people and populations. This can include (but not limited to) **age, sex, class, nationality, geographic location.**

**BENEFITS**: Understanding your demographic goes hand in hand with customer research. The data collected through demographics helps businesses to **understand how to market to consumers** and **plan strategically for future trends in consumer demand.**

# DIVISION OF LABOUR

The division of labour is essentially what it says it is - the separation of tasks within a business. Having people who are specialised at a certain field working on that field and aspect of the business. For example, you would want a business manager to run and manage the business. You would want someone who is specialised in advertising to do marketing for your business.

**BENEFITS:** The business is ***running effectively*** and will perform so much better. You will have ***increased group cohesion***. You are dividing the workload, which will ***increase people's wellbeing***. You are also ***utilising your team members to the fullest*** of their abilities.

**BOSSNOTE:** A lot of entrepreneurs believe they have to be the jack of all trades and spend their time trying to master a multitude of skills. This normally results in mastering none of them.
You are far better building your team of specialised individuals who play their own specific roles in the business. I appreciate when you're initially starting a business you're starting from the ground and a lot of the elements of the business will be run by yourself.

My advice is as soon as you can outsource, DO! It frees up more time for you to work on the things which will take your business to the next level, i.e the quality of your product or the quality of service which you provide.
You also have to accept that…**YOU CAN'T BE THE BEST AT EVERYTHING.**
Focused energy is better than scattered energy.

# DEEP DIVE

When a business starts facing continual problems, it's time to take a deep dive into the business to identify, analyse and then to mitigate negatives in an efficient manner.

During deep dives, you will find **BLIND SPOTS** in your business, places that haven't been optimized and given the care needed to ensure the business is making maximum profits. Issues that have slipped under the radar.

**BENEFITS:** Deep diving allows the business to operate in the most *risk-averse way possible.*

**BOSSNOTE:** Although many businesses wait until problems start to arrive before they take a deep dive, you as an entrepreneur should be taking deep dives monthly! It will save you a tremendous amount of *time*, *money* and *energy*.

# DISTRIBUTION

Distribution is the process of making a product and delivery of service to the **consumer** or business user who needs it. Distribution can occur directly by the producer, service provider, or even by the use of indirect channels with distributors or intermediaries.

# DELIVERABLE

A thing able to be provided, especially as a product of a development process. When you provide a deliverable, you are essentially providing a third party with the details of the service that they are going to provide you with or 'deliver' to you.

If you are in the online world, you would have or will come across this word. For example, if you want a graphic produced by a freelancer you will need to provide the deliverable, which entails, colour, size, time frame to complete the project, ideas of what you want the logo to look like. Then they will deliver you the product using the deliverable information you have provided them.

**BOSS NOTE:** This one is simple. Be clear, concise and keep things very simple.

# EXIT CRITERIA

Exit criteria are the criteria or requirements which must be met to complete a specific task or process as used in some fields of business or science.
Exit criteria is mainly applied in software engineering.

**Benefits:**

Ensures **customers satisfaction**

It helps achieve **technical excellence**

It make the development process **simple and straightforward** to follow

# EVANGELISM MARKETING

Evangelism marketing is a fancy way of describing word-of-mouth marketing, which customers openly partake in constantly.

Certain businesses have an incredible relationship with their customers who believe so strongly in a particular product or service that they freely try to convince others to buy and use it. This is essentially a referral scheme without payment for the referral. The customers become voluntary advocates, actively promoting your business's service or product.

**BENEFITS:** Allows for cheaper marketing. You have people who are increasing your brand awareness. You are getting more sales, and an increased consumer base. Having an evangelist as a customer is simply one of the most powerful assets you can have in your business.

**BOSSNOTE:** This varies from business to business. Some businesses have more evangelist marketers than others. In my humble opinion, the best way to harness this amazing form of marketing is by focusing your energy on satisfying and solving your customer's deepest needs and problems, providing exemplary customer service, and finally, nurturing and building a strong relationship with them.

# EVALUATION

A business evaluation is an analysis and review of a business entity. This tends to occur when a business owner wants to sell the business. The evaluation gives overall standing and operation. These are vital pieces of information a buyer would want to know, as it helps them gain a better understanding of what areas may need attention and what changes need to be implemented to get the results desired from the purchase.

### Things included during the evaluation process:

Sales, products, services, marketing strategy, business activity, customer relationships (whether there's an established community or not), location…

**BENEFITS:** If you have a great evaluation = *LOTS AND LOTS OF F\*CKING MONEY.*

**BOSS NOTE:** These are variables sensible buyers will look at. When I have bought a business, the main thing I'm looking at is marketing strategy, and whether or not the business has a strong community. The rest I have strong belief I can fix. If you have a strong community, believe me when I say you can monetize if you're ***creative***.

*I'm grateful to have a team of extremely creative and passionate individuals.*

## So, how does this help you?

Focus on building relationships and communities.
Focus on the variables which are outlined above.
If you're building a business (which I assume you are as you've purchased this book), somewhere down the line you may want to sell it. Start now, to think about all the variables within your business and create value, and work very hard to increase the value of each aspect. Don't sleep on it, form it as a habit early on. Even if you never want to sell it, focusing on these variables is what makes the business succeed.

**MAKE SURE YOUR BUSINESS IS BUYABLE.**

# EARNED MEDIA

Earned media this refers to publicity gained through promotional efforts other than paid media advertising. Earned media included the publicity gained through advertising. Businesses have to spend the time and energy required to build strong relationships with your customers and brand advocates.

**BENEFITS**: Earned media is proven to have *better ROI* and is also more *cost effective.*

## ENTREPRENEUR

### YOU!

### Write what this means to you.

# FUNNEL

The sales funnel, also known as a revenue funnel or the sales process, refers to the buying process which customers go through when purchasing products.

The process of a funnel is as follows: find a buyer, qualify the buyer (make sure the product is sold to the right person), sell the product to the buyer (purchase).

An easier way to see this is as the journey the customer takes from point of entry (when they were first initially exposed to the product, to when they finally purchase the product and become a customer.

Or, the sequence of steps the customer had to take to purchase the product. This process is almost always subdivided into different stages.

## An example of a funnel for an online course could go as follows:

Sees an ad, clicks it

Get taken to online seminar and watches 'webinar'
End of webinar: gets taken to landing page
Purchases product at landing page.

It's important to note that the funnel process varies and is drastically different for each business and business models. So, like much of the processes outlined in this book, there is no one size fits all approach. Each sales funnel should be personalised and uniquely designed with appreciation of the business type, and the target market/ideal customer.

**BENEFITS:** *Every single activity is tracked* during the sales process which means you are more accountable. You can *easily spot weak areas* in the funnel process that need more attention.

### If you have a great funnel:
Conversion rates drastically increase

More accurate predictions can be made about sales

Increases revenue of the business

Makes marketing easier

## FOUNDERS

Founders are the individuals who established the business. They are the individuals who created something from nothing.

# FREEMIUM

This is a common practice in which start-ups offer a free plan to customers which include product features, while trying to encourage subscribers to upgrade their plans to a more attractive offer.
An example of this would be Youtube; of course we have a free plan but they try to upsell us to their premium plan which means no targeted ads, more premium content made by youtube, offline watching, downloadable videos and music. Maybe even more.

Businesses try to make their premium offer as attractive as they can so it's a no brainer for the customer to buy the upgraded plan!

**BENEFITS:** The freemium model is a *great way to get the attention* of potential customers using the 'FREE TAG'. This of course *increases your product and brand awareness* as you have more eyes on your product. Freemiums also mean you are able to *upsell customers*, and is a great way to increase business revenue.

# FINANCIAL SYSTEM

The collective bodies which make money move around the world. Governments, businesses, cooperations, banks, consumers and producer. We are all part and parcel of the financial system.

# FREE TRADE

Free trade, also known as open trade, is the arrangement that countries are allowed to freely trade with each other without any legal constraints. The first free trade agreement was signed in 1860, between England and France.

Free trade is measured by the volume of exports and imports of countries.

**BENEFITS:** Free trade means we get *lowered prices for consumers*, it *increases economic value* of countries and you have a *wider range of goods* to choose from.

# FINANCIAL PROJECTION

This is the process in which a business uses collected data and evaluation of external market variables to make a prediction of future revenues and expenses.

Most businesses account for both short term and long term financial projections. This gives businesses the forethought to better appoint their resources and allows for preparations.

# FRANCHISE

Franchising is defined as an agreement or license between two legally independent parties which gives: A person or group of people (the franchisee) the right to market a product or service using the trademark or trade name of another business (the franchisor).

**(Standardised definition)**

Therefore, a business which allows the process to take place is known as a franchise.

Here are some common franchises:

McDonald's

Subway

Domino's

Taco Bell

**BENEFITS:**

Speed of growth

Increased capital

Increased brand equity

Limited risk and liability

Cheaper advertising and promotions

Decreased involvement in the day to day operation

Motivated and effective management

## Benefits Of 'Joining' A Franchise Chain:

You have the advantage of **operating under the name** of a very **popular** and well **respected business.**

Most of the work has been done for you in terms of the **brand awareness** and **customer acquisition process.**

You have a great **support system.**

You **build strong business relationships.**

Defeats the odds that businesses fail within the first 5 years.

## DRAWBACKS:

**You don't have full control** of the business

You are **tied to certain suppliers** which the franchise has formed.

You are **gambling that the brand reputation** will hold up.

Franchises require a **large** amount of **capital to start.**

You will be charged a **'franchise fee'.**

It can be **difficult to exit** the business.

# FRANCHISE-ABLE BUSINESS

As we have already discussed what a franchise is, here are the characteristics of a franchise-able business.

**Barrier to entry:**

The business must be *established*. The business must offer a *unique idea* or concept. The business must be teachable. This business must be able to *provide adequate returns* to the potential franchisee.

# FULFILMENT

This is the closing achievement/completion of a deal, once it is agreed.

# FUNDAMENTALS

This is the necessary foundation which must be built for a business to strive and succeed. Fundamentals of a business are tied to the business model, so they can differ from business to business. However, there are also overarching fundamentals to business as a whole, such as supply and demand.

**BOSSNOTE:** Depending on what business you want to start, make sure you assess the business fundamentals. Assess variables which need attention to ensure you have the best chance of succeeding in your particular business. Many people getting into business think it's a straightforward path, not fully understanding what makes their type of business successful. Is it customer service? Is it the product itself? Is it brand awareness?

Ask yourself the question: what are the most basic things that I need to fulfil every time with this business that if I don't, would lead to the collapse of the business?

**Answer these questions and you have the fundamentals to your business.**

# FIRST MOVER ADVANTAGE

A first mover advantage is a term which is used to describe the inherent advantage a business or individual has over their competitors as a result of being first to market in a new product category. Due to the fact they are first in the market potential customers have one option to go to, to get the product or service which the first mover business provides.

This is also advantageous as the business is able to get a head start in customer acquisition, customer research and branding.

**BOSSNOTE:** It must be said that this doesn't always guarantee success. The success of the business is down to the ability and execution of the first mover business. If a second business opens up in the same category and is able to provide a better service or higher quality product, they are more likely to succeed.

# GOLDEN STANDARD

This is the reference point for the highest quality standard at which a service or product should be provided. Golden standard helps businesses consistently produce and deliver the best quality service.

# GLOBALIZATION

Globalization is a term that refers to the trend for people, firms and governments around the world to become increasingly dependent on and integrated with one another. Globalization also refers to the process in which a business grows to a point where they gain international influence, meaning they can operate at a global scale.

There are three types of globalisation, *economic, cultural and political globalisation.*

We are mainly focusing on **economic globalisation.**

**Benefits:**

More money

Increased opportunity

Access to infinite market

An ever expanding brand awareness

Increased workers, customers, business partnerships, goods and services.

GROWTH

Simply put, this is the process in which a business increases in size. Growth in a business is usually measured using certain metrics.

**Sales, revenue, client base, number of customers, number of workers, increased cash flow and diverse audience base.**

**BOSSNOTE:** The golden indicator of growth for you will be HATERS. Believe it or not, when you start to evolve and level up as an entrepreneur you will start receiving more negative reception. Ignore the haters and keep doing your thing. Haters unfortunately come hand in hand with progress and success! Trust me!

# GOING PRIVATE

If a business is going private this means it is closing the door to all future potential.

# GROWTH HACKING

Growth hacking is the process by which an entrepreneur uses unconventional strategies (these tend to be unique and creative) to drastically increase growth of a business at a cost that is significantly lower than the 'average' amount which would normally be required to attain the same results.

This is what a successful marketing campaign should aim to do.

**BENEFITS:**

Cost effective

Increased marketing effectiveness (scalable marketing)

Embraces the growth mentality

Encourages creative thinking

All of these benefits translate to *more money*

**BOSSNOTE:** You as an entrepreneur should always be thinking of unique marketing strategies your business can incorporate. Doing so differentiates you from the market. It makes you unique, it also means your business will have absolute advantage over other similar businesses in your market. I personally am constantly thinking and encouraging my workers to think in this way. You need to stand out from the saturated market.

# HAGGLE

Haggling is the process of negotiation between two parties on a fair price for a service or product.

**BOSSNOTE:** This is a skill which you will develop over time. Unfortunately, the only teacher on how to properly haggle is experience. Experience is after all our best teacher.

# HALO EFFECT

This entails a consumer who now has a bias and favoritism towards a line of products due to previous positive experiences with the product or service. The halo effect strongly tied with a brand's strength and loyalty, and contributes to brand equity.

# HUMAN CAPITAL

Human capital is the stock of habits, knowledge, social and personality attributes (including creativity) embodied in the ability to perform labour so as to produce value. Human capital can also be seen as the economic value of a worker's experience and skills.

**BOSSNOTE:** Make sure you invest in your worker, education, skills and health training. Doing so will increase the inherent value of your business. Although you should try saving where you can, it is also important to recognise the importance of spending and investing into your own education as well as your team's. So when that time comes, don't hesitate.

# INBOUND MARKETING

This is a unique business strategy which aims to attract new customers by creating free high quality content that is valuable to the customer's experience and is tailored to them. Although inbound marketing can be very time consuming if you are just starting off a business, it is of the utmost importance as an extremely effective way of marketing which yields high returns long term.

## Here are a few examples of different forms of inbound marketing:

Customer guides

Educational videos

Free training programmes

Podcasts

Infographics

To give a better overview of the method that inbound tries to follow: You attract your potential customer (via targeted ads, video, blogs, social media), following this you continue to *engage* with that potential customer (via, email, messenger, lead flows or marketing automations), then finally you *consistently delight* that potential customer giving and providing them with freebies and important valuable content which they would appreciate. For example, if your target audience was podcasters, you would frequently make video blogs on how they can solve the 'marketing problem' increasing their number of listeners, what the best practices are when starting a podcast.

**BOSSNOTE:** The very important thing about inbound marketing is that it is done *consistently over a long period of time*. You need to ensure you are *constantly pumping out great value*, and more importantly *helpful content* which your audience/potential customer is likely to need and engage with. You are trying to *build a strong* *relationship* with these individuals, so although *it is hard work* and frankly *tedious* at times especially when you're just starting off and you have no other people working in your team, it can feel overwhelming trying to keep up with things. Trust me, I know. Whilst acknowledging this, I must say that once executed, *inbound marketing yields tremendous rewards for* your *brand* and *customer base*.

**Inbound marketing forms connections they are looking for and solves problems they already have.**

# INTERACTION DESIGN

This is the way your website is designed. Interaction design has the user in mind and tries to ensure that the website is as easy to use as possible. I.e, it's user friendly.

**BENEFITS:** Having a great interaction design *increases website activity* as people do browse through. You have a great design to your website and it gives it a *professional feel* which has been *proven to convert more leads* (potential buyers). Having a more user friendly design also *increases traffic to your website* and *helps you rank* well in search engines. Finally, having a great design is also one of the *most powerful ways to market your brand.*

**BOSSNOTE:** If you're an entrepreneur looking to get into the online world, user interaction design is something that should be in the forefront of your mind. Scrap that, if you're an entrepreneur period, this is something you shouldn't overlook.

# IMPORTS

This is the purchase of foreign goods and services and is the opposite of export.

# INCUMBENT ADVANTAGE

This is typically a business term used to express the advantage that a firm/business already established in the market has advantage over a new business coming into the market. This is due to the fact the business which possesses an incumbent advantage has a settled place in the market.

**BENEFITS:** Having incumbent advantage means a business is **able to generate higher profits** than a new firm (an entrant) even if the entrant offers identical terms to consumers, or even better terms in terms of **price, quality, customer base, and opportunity** due to the already formed network/relationships with other businesses in the market.

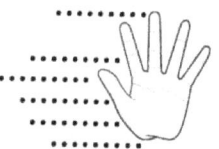

# INVISIBLE HAND EFFECT

***'The unobservable market force that helps the demand and supply of goods in a free market to reach equilibrium automatically is the invisible hand.'*** This is the official definition of the invisible hand effect.

You can also see the invisible hand affect the forces which can't be directly seen but that are constantly working in your favour to get more sales or get more clients. For example, if you are constantly providing value for free to your audience, although there is no direct gain from this, in the background you are cementing your brand in their mind and if your product ever came up in conversation they would be the first to recommend it to their friend.

A perfect example of this is how you never directly see evangelists for your business, but they are constantly there in the background working, promoting and spreading the word about your business. It's important to note that the invisible hand effect using my definition can have a positive effect or negative effect, depending on how well you run your business.

If you run a great business, the invisible hand effect will be working in your favor. If you run a bad business, the invisible hand works against you.

# INNOVATION

Business innovation is when a business or an individual introduces new processes, services, or products, which has a positive effect on their business. This can include improving existing methods or practices, or starting from scratch.

**BENEFITS:** This can give you a ***competitive advantage*** in the market. Innovation allows for significant improvement of systems and can lead to a large amount of ***money being saved***, meaning more money for the business and increased capital.

# INTELLECTUAL CAPITAL

Intellectual capital is seen as human ideas rather than physical ideas. Intellectual capital essentially means how valuable are your human assets in regards to creative process and problem solving.

Most of the time when you have intellectual capital you are able to get the ideas protected through a patent/trademark. This protects your ideas from being stolen, and gives complete ownership of that particular idea. Now, other businesses or individuals are allowed to commercially monetize this idea.

Intellectual capital is also seen as an **INTANGIBLE ASSET.**

# INVENTORY

An inventory is the goods available for sale and the raw materials which are used to produce the goods, merchandise and material available.

Most businesses own an inventory which is seen as one of the most important assets that a business can have. If you have a high turnover inventory, you are able to clear your inventory quickly in a short period of time.

This directly correlates to the amount of revenue that your business is able to generate.

**BENEFITS:** A business can use the information which can be collected by the inventory turnover time (how long it takes for the entire inventory to be used up), to make an ***educated examination/decision of pricing of product, manufacturing marketing*** and whether or not they will need to invest in a new inventory. Having an inventory also ***reduces your risk of over selling*** as you have a knowledge of what you have left and are able to deliver to the market. Having this collected data also ***improves your business negotiation*** when it comes to building partnerships and eventually when it comes to selling your business.

# INVESTMENT

In simple terms, an investment is the act of putting money into something in the hopes that in the future that money will grow and be of better value than the initial investment.

There are two forms of investment; direct investments which is spending on buildings, machinery, business etc... and indirect investing, where you are putting money in bonds and shares.

A keyword in this is that you invest in hopes. Of course there are ways to invest and reduce your risk of losing the investment; in doing so increases your chance of getting positive returns. The easiest way to manage risk is doing thorough research on what it is you want to invest into. This means you are able to make an educated decision on whether or not to invest.

**BENEFITS:**

Earn additional income

Beat inflation

Greater opportunity to make money through compound effects

**BOSSNOTE:** The best thing that you can invest in is yourself. So, begin to invest in yourself by reading books like these, which are vital for the success of an aspiring entrepreneur. Applied knowledge is power. You should also start investing in your health and mental wellbeing. These are all things which require no extra cost. I.e, begin to meditate for your mental wellbeing, and start choosing to exercise whether that is working out or going to a gym.

You have to be strong and healthy in mind, body and spirit.

# JOB

**Definition: a thing all entrepreneurs hate and would never have permanently.**

**We don't work jobs, we create jobs.**

# KNOWLEDGE

Facts, information, and skills acquired through experience or education; the theoretical or practical understanding of a subject.

**BOSSNOTE:** The more knowledge which you are able to acquire in relation to your business, the better off you will be.

# LEVERAGE

Leverage is seen as the acquiring of debt or the purpose of making an investment.

For something to be highly leveraged, the item has more debt than it does equity. The concept of leverage is heavily used by both investors and companies.

You are able to leverage assets.

# LIQUIDITY

Liquidity is a term used to describe how easily an asset can be spent (converted to real cash), if so desired.

Cash is wholly liquid.

When an asset is converted to real cash or money in your pocket that means the asset is liquidated.

---

**BENEFITS:** If something has a high liquidity, it means it can easily be converted to cash. This is very attractive to a lot of people as some people in times of emergency can easily liquidate an asset if they need to. It provides convenience for the asset holder.

# LIMITED LIABILITY COMPANY

This business is a separate entity to its owner, meaning that the owners are not personally liable for the business debt or liability.

**General Process Of Forming An LLC:**

Choose a name for your LLC

Choose a registered agent

Decide on member vs. manager management

Prepare an operating agreement

File biennial report

Pay your tax obligations

Comply with other tax and regulatory requirements

# LOGISTICS

The detailed organization and implementation of a complex operation.

This term is widely in the business sector and mainly refers to how resources are handled.

I personally view this as a breakdown of all the important aspects of a business, and how an operation is handled.

# LONG TERMS

I'm sure you know the definition of long term, I just put it in here because this is how you should train your mind to think. Long term not short term. You must constantly be factoring the future to make decisions in the present far more manageable. You must have a long term view of your business and understand you should always act in accordance to things that will benefit you long term. This is a rule that applies heavily to all aspects.

**Live not for instant gratification, but for delayed gratification.**

Time can either work for you or against you. I am always excited about the future because I am spending my time wisely in the present. I have built the foundations and the more time goes by, the closer I get to my goals to my ambitions, the closer I get to becoming a fully realised entrepreneur.

A person who wants to be successful would be excited about the future, not worried or scared.

If you find that you are currently worried about the future and you are feeling unsure, take time right now to reflect and understand the deep rooted reasons as to why you feel worried.

We are problem solvers, that's what makes us so functional and adaptive. We solve problems whether that's business or internal problems we may face.

MONEY

Is not the root of happiness, living a fulfilled life is. Money is a means to live a more free life, whilst at the same time can enslave those who aren't careful. You should always make money work for you, not the other way round.

---

# MONETIZE

This is the process in which an item that is non-revenue can be converted into cash, you can see this as the process of liquidating an asset.

To monetize is to liquidate an asset.

# MANUFACTURING

Manufacturing is the process by which goods are created by hand or machine. These goods tend to come from raw materials or component parts of a larger product. This process occurs on a large scale, in combination with many machines and labour workers.

# MANAGEMENT

**The process by which you deal with people or things.**

**BENEFITS:**

Deliver work on time
Produce higher quality of work
More productivity and efficiency
Decreased procrastination
Less stress and anxiety
Improved quality of life
More opportunities and career growth
More time for leisure and recreation

**BOSS NOTE:** I personally believe that having great time management is one of the most important things when it comes to being a successful entrepreneur.

This is a skill that must be developed over time and through practice, patience and experience.

I'm sure you would have heard the saying that we all have 24 hours in a day; it's what we chose to do with those hours that makes the difference.

Well this statement is true in more ways than one. When I was first dreaming about making millions, I would spend too much time thinking, when I should have been planning and acting. Through planning and acting you can gain a better understanding of what you are able to accomplish in a day.

As you go through your own personal journey, humans have a tendency to undershoot how long tasks will take, so always be conservative when you are setting goals and creating plans.

# NETWORK

Networking is simply the exchange of information and ideas among people with a common profession or interest, usually in an informal social setting.
You can network with people who are in the same market as you to find out information about things they do, systems they have set up to make certain processes easier.

**NETWORK MARKETING:** This is a business model which is heavily dependent on the one to one interactions of individuals and representatives of a business who form a network of people, mainly online, to try and generate sales. Although it can be great, in many network markets people only really get paid for each person who is recruited to the network rather than the sale of a product. Through these many network markets experience the **NETWORK EFFECT;** where by due to the increased number of individuals in the network, the group service or value see great improvement.

**BOSSNOTE:** Networking is part of our everyday lives. We are constantly involved with networks, with our friends, families, colleagues. It's just unconscious networking.

The real power comes from purposeful networking. When you first start a business, it is integral that you network heavy; I mean you have to reach out to hundreds of people each week (if not thousands); this can be done online, where you might have to live in your potential customer's platform and create a network, or even where your competitors or other business minded people are. Your aim should be to form a solid relationship with people by just being there, checking up on them and asking questions. This is how most businesses start. Once you form a network of people you trust, everything in your business becomes easier. You have the support for your customers and you have the guidance of your competitors who have walked a similar path to you.

# OPTIMUM

Optimum means to perform at the highest quality, or for something to conduct at a favorable outcome.

For something to be optimized, changes are being made to the system or process to allow it to work in a more favorable way.

### Optimizing can take different forms, which are all BENEFICIAL:

The introduction of a new more efficient method

Changes practices within the workplace

Creating automated systems that run faster

The reduction of cost whilst still maintaining the same or increased performance

**BOSSNOTE:** You are just coming into the entrepreneur space; just know that this is a word that will often come up and something that you should always be thinking about; what changes can you make to ensure your business is working as efficiently as possible? It's important to note that optimization mainly comes in the form of improving ad campaigns. My main optimization occurs with the ads I run, I try to get my cost down and either maintain or even increase performance.

You need to start identifying and implementing new things in your business which can bring it closer to the optimum.

Things might be going well, but can almost always be better. You should always have this progressive mindset. You should always be building momentum as an entrepreneur. It is those who master this skill, knowing they have much power to put on the gas are the ones who succeed. But just like a lot of things which I have mentioned in the bossnotes, it doesn't come without practice and nurturing of the particular skill, this is no different.

# OBLIGATIONS

This is seen as a course of action which an individual has to perform due to morally or legally binding reasons. It can also be seen as a person's duty to perform a certain task.

**BOSSNOTE:** For you some obligations may come under planning, management, organization, representation and networking and of course, the development of your business.

Most start-ups have an obligation to give their business time and energy.

# OPPORTUNITY

Opportunities are seen as a set of often unlikely circumstances that makes something possible.

An example would be an aspiring artist bumping into a record label that they have always wanted to meet and interact with.

**BENEFITS:** They provide us with a particular situations which we are able to seize and make the best out of. Opportunity gives us a chance to make our dreams, goals and greatest ambitions some true.

**BOSSNOTE**: You can create opportunities for yourself through taking consistent action. If you start, every action you take in your business will create an equal opportunity for you somewhere in the future if you keep working hard and staying consistent with your work. Too many people sit about waiting for the right opportunity to execute a business plan or to start working on a new project. The truth of the matter is there are no such things.

You create your own chance/luck in life, you are in control and no external forces enforce opportunity on you but yourself. You can train yourself to spot opportunities and it's a skill every person, not just entrepreneurs, should try to develop. I have gone through some transformative changes over the last year or two and being able to spot opportunities has become a thing that is more frequent. Then again, it's down to the fact I have trained myself to always see situations as an opportunity.

Each interaction you have in this world is an opportunity whether you know it or not - it might be made evident instantly, or it might take months or maybe even years.

It's important not to get caught up in opportunities; as I said, you can generate opportunity at any time, the important part is can you train yourself to execute once you're at that point.

Like the man Conor McGregor said: 'It's a beautiful feeling when preparation meets opportunity'.

# OUTSOURCE

This is the process in which a business pays an outside supplier to produce goods, write books, design ad banners, or work on a service which the business themselves aren't directly linked to.

**BENEFITS:** It allows you to **keep your focus on the core business activity.** Outsourcing is also a great way to **help aspiring freelancers** make some extra money. It always provides a means for you to **grow your network and build relationships** with people outside of your close business circle, in turn potentially leading to the **development of your internal staff**. Outsourcing is an amazing way to **save time,** allowing you to focus on more important work that yields the most/best results for your business. Outsourcing always tends to be cheap, which in turn can **lower the cost of your business.**

**BOSSNOTE:** Outsourcing is a very important part of most businesses, and I truly believe if you are able to outsource things in your business you should, as it's mostly beneficial for both parties for the reasons stated above.

However, when you are starting a business, the initial thoughts are to save money and try to do these things yourself which is completely fine. Just have the recognition that once you are making enough money with the business to accelerate the process, you can outsource some services. This will help you in turn as you will get quality services through outsourcing which will help the quality of your business and the professionalism of your brand.

# PROFIT MARGIN

This represents the number of sales in a business which turn into profit.

# PROPERTY

A property is a thing which belongs to someone. If you have property, that is legally yours and you own it.

**Here are the three different forms of property**

Private

Public

Collective

# PIVOT

To pivot means that a business is going to change and move to a new strategy, often meaning significant changes will be made in order to prompt positive improvement.

### Different examples of what a pivot may entail:

Targeting a different demographic

Changing the main platform

The adoption of a new business model to increase monetization

The integration of advanced technology

The conversion of featured products as actual products and assets for a business

### Bossnote:

### Ways to effectively pivot:

Get on the *pivot early* on when you are aware of this being a possibility

Ensure that the **new goal** which you have for your business still **aligns with your vision**

You **don't have to completely eliminate your old model**, just take influence and inspiration from areas that did work and areas that didn't that you can scrap

Be an **active listener to your customer** and they will direct you in the right path. They have all your answers - again, this links closely to why knowing your customer is so important

Analyse and evaluate the pivot strategy to ensure that it **allows for scalability and massive growth.**

# PRICE DISCOVERY

This is seen as the process in which the price of an asset is being determined by the market. This is a process which is heavily influenced by the interaction of buyers and sellers.

This is a word most traders will be familiar with.

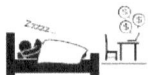

# PASSIVE INCOME

Passive income is earnings derived from a rental property, limited partnership, or other enterprise in which a person is not actively involved.

**BOSSNOTE:** Passive income is known in our community as the promised land.

# PERCEIVED VALUE

Perceived value is your customer's subjective view of your product or the services which the business provides. Perceived value is formed by the comparison of your products/services quality to that of a competitor's.

Perceived value is measured by the price the public is willing to pay for goods or services.

**BOSSNOTE:** It is fair to say that at times, the perceived value of your product outweighs the actual value of your product. This is okay, as the aim is for the perceived value to be as high as possible to result in as many sales as possible, while still being genuinely valuable.

# PATENT

A patent is the legal ownership of an invention, meaning no one else is allowed to take your idea and make money from it.

**BENEFITS**: Having a **patent** means you have the right to stop others from copying, manufacturing, selling or importing your invention without your permission. This means by law, you are able to protect your intellectual property.

# PRODUCTIVITY

In a more literal sense, productivity is associated with the output and input volume. This essentially means the direct measurement of the efficiency of production input, including labour and capital used to produce a certain amount of output of a product.

In terms of productivity on an individual level, it still follows the same principles as the definition stated above. You can view productivity as how much quality work you are able to produce in a period of time. If you're being very productive in your business it means you are putting out the best quality of work in a highly time efficient way.

**BENEFITS:** You are able to ***complete quality work in a short period of time***. You are able to comfortably ***take on more challenging tasks*** with more confidence compared to a person who isn't as productive. Being productive also means you are ***moving on to your next task at a faster rate.***

**BOSSNOTE:** As entrepreneurs, we are always trying to find ways to increase productivity, to increase how much we can accomplish in a day. This is an ongoing process and one that requires time spent practicing different techniques and figuring out which one works for you.

### Here are simple ways to increase productivity:

When you're working, get rid of your phone

Set a daily goal, weekly goal and monthly goal to help you stay on track

Tackle the most important tasks earlier in the day

Wake up earlier

Have routine breaks from work, e.g 20 minutes on, 5 minutes off

# PYRAMID SCHEME

Pyramid schemes are chain referral schemes - marketing and investment frauds in which an individual is offered a distributorship or franchise to market a particular product. Profits are earned not by the sale of a product, but by the sale of new distributorships

**BOSSNOTE: These are completely illegal and you should avoid them at all cost.**

I very nearly fell for this in my early years when I was trying to discover what to do with myself.

# QUALITY CONTROL

Quality control is a process through which a business tries to ensure that product quality is maintained or improved.

For great quality control, a business must create an environment in which both management and employees strive for excellence.

# QUALITY OF LIFE

This is seen as the measure of a person's **health, wealth, comfort**, and the level of **happiness experienced** by a person.

**BOSSNOTE**: The benefits of this one are probably clear. We all want to be happy in life, this is probably the part where I express to you that money is not going to buy you happiness. I lie, it will buy you happiness, but only to the extent that it provides you with a good quality life in terms of wealth and comfort…and health if you use it correctly.

You have to understand your quality of life isn't dependent on money and it shouldn't be. Money is an added bonus and a means to experience new things that you otherwise would not have been able to.

What point am I trying to make?

In your pursuit for success via means of running a successful business, if you find that you are losing or sacrificing your mental wellbeing and have stopped enjoying your work, I urge you to reflect and understand that you should always put your quality of life first.

Remember that there **is** such a thing as toxic positivity.

# REVENUE

Revenue is seen as the total amount of money a business is able to generate in a year. Revenue doesn't take cost into account, so it's not a reflection of profits.

# RESIDUAL INCOME

This is seen as the income you will continue to receive once you have done the work for an income producing system.

**Residual income include:**

Building an online course

Working as an affiliate

Selling a design

Writing a book

Creating an app

Rental/real estate income

Interest earned from shares and bonds

Dividends paid to yourself from your business

**BENEFITS:** You do the work upfront and get paid continually month after month. It's thinking long term.

**BOSSNOTE:** I hope this example has made the idea and definition more clear in your mind. You can see residual income as the money you receive after you complete a piece of work that can continually pay you in the future - not just a one off payment, but an ongoing one that isn't completely passive, but let's say semi passive.

## STOCK/SHARES

Is seen as quality which is held by an individual which represents the fraction of a corporation of business they hold.

# STRATEGIC ALLIANCE

A strategic alliance is an arrangement which is reached between two businesses. This allows for mutual benefits to the projects they work on, individually or collaboratively. Strategic alliances are different to joint ventures.

Joint ventures draw businesses' pooled resources to **create an entirely separate business entity.**

**BENEFITS:** Strategic alliance means you have access to a whole new client base and customers. You are able to easily insert yourself into a new business sector and advance your business prowess with the help of your alliance. You are able to create more income producing resources. You have increased risk management. You combine a pool of creative minds with your workers and allow for innovation to take place.

**BOSSNOTE:** Through networking, you are able to constantly form professional strategic alliances in whatever business you're in. I've said it through this book: the most important things in business are the relationships you build and form with people in your market space.

It's like the saying: 'It's not what you know, it's who you know'.

# SYSTEMIC RISK

This underlines the possibility that a dramatic event can occur in a business which causes severe instability and can lead to the end of said business.

# TREND

**The general direction in which something is developing or changing.**

**BOSSNOTE:** As an aspiring entrepreneur, you should be always looking for the trends in the market and seeing where you can jump in to make a profit.

# TOXIC POSITIVITY

We define toxic positivity as the excessive and ineffective overgeneralization of a happy, optimistic state across all situations. The process of toxic positivity results in the denial, minimization, and invalidation of the authentic human emotional experience.

**BOSSNOTE:** I hate to say it, but this is heavily encouraged in the self-help community and by the image of what an entrepreneur should be like. It is overly popularised that you have to be constantly positive which naturally means mutes negative emotions. Studies have actually shown this can be detrimental to your wellbeing as suppressing feelings can cause more internal, psychological stress.

You also have to recognize that all humans go through some very tough patches in their journey to success. It's important not to withhold your emotions but rather give yourself time to feel the emotion, internalize it, then once you have reflected, thinking of an active way to regain control and to be proactive about your problems and move on. Having a positive attitude is important but at the same time, don't force positivity on to yourself all the time.

# WEALTH EFFECT

This occurs when you become wealthier and consume more.

# BURNOUT

Burnout is a state of emotional, physical, and mental exhaustion caused by excessive and prolonged stress. It occurs when you feel overwhelmed, emotionally drained, and unable to meet constant demands.

**BENEFITS: This is clearly a negative thing.**

**BOSSNOTE:**

This is a lot more common than you might think, and although you should have the hustle mentality deep in you, you also need to have a good gage of when burnout is creeping in. There is literally no point in getting yourself burnt out as it's counterproductive and a hindrance to you achieving your goals.

## Here are some practical steps to take to avoid getting burnt out:

Have a healthy balanced work schedule
Take control back in your life (this can be done just by writing a simple timetable for your day, which has been proven to increase the sense of control in your life)

Having a nap. I know right, the only time you'll be advised to nap on a job ;) Seriously, naps are great for releasing tension and helping you stay focused and attentive.

Please do share with the group your story if you have experienced burnout and how you dealt with it. Spreading awareness can help us all move forward.

## FINAL BOSSNOTE:

I would like to say thank you for purchasing this book. I hope you got a great insight and a broadened understanding of key business terminology.

On a more personal level, I want to let you know that no matter where you find yourself in life, no matter how good or bad the situation, always take time to reflect and always understand that you are in full control of your life.

Life will always challenge you, as will business - it's just the yin and yang. So when the going gets tough, make sure to keep going and push past resistance, as this is the barrier to entry of success.

Love from a fellow adaptive individual.